The Fen And Marshland Churches, A Ser. Of Photogr.,with Short Historical And Architectural Descriptive Notes. The Photogr. Illustr. By E. Johnson...

Fen and marshland churches, Edward Johnson (illustrator.)

THE FEN AND MARSHLAND CHURCHES.

(THIRD SERIES.)

CROYLAND.

THE

FEN AND MARSHLAND

CHURCHES;

A SERIES OF PHOTOGRAPHS,

WITH SHORT

HISTORICAL AND ARCHITECTURAL
DESCRIPTIVE NOTES, & GROUND PLANS.

THIRD SERIES.

WISBECH :
LEACH AND SON, 26, HIGH STREET.

LONDON :
SIMPKIN, MARSHALL AND CO., STATIONERS' HALL COURT, E.C.

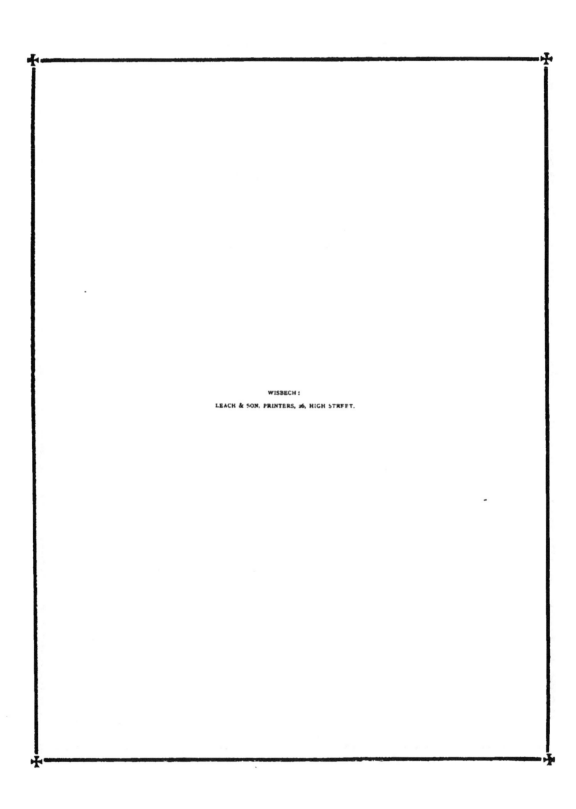

WISBECH:

LEACH & SON, PRINTERS, 26, HIGH STREET.

TO

THE RIGHT REVEREND

JOHN

LORD BISHOP OF LONDON,

AND TO

THE RIGHT REVEREND

CHRISTOPHER,

LORD BISHOP OF LINCOLN,

THIS VOLUME

IS

BY THEIR LORDSHIPS' PERMISSION

RESPECTFULLY DEDICATED

BY THEIR OBLIGED AND OBEDIENT SERVANTS,

LEACH & SON.

CONTENTS.

PHOTOGRAPHIC ILLUSTRATIONS.

BY EDWARD JOHNSON.

BOSTON.

S. BOTOLPH'S, BOSTON, LINCOLNSHIRE.

"THE Chirche of S. Botolph" says Leland in his Itinerary, "is now so risen and adornid that it is the chiefest in the towne and for a paroche Chirche *the best and fayrest of all Lincolnshire.*" It is no purpose of the present sketch to decide whether this preference for the Church of Boston over its "fayre" rivals, more especially the sister Churches of Grantham and Louth, be a just judgement or a mere personal prejudice. Probably the true estimate to be formed of their respective claims to superiority is that each has its own distinctive excellence and possesses features of interest which the others lack. In point of size, however, (for it

B

is the largest in England without transepts) and in simplicity of design and beauty of proportion, above all in its stupendous tower and unrivalled lantern, S. Botolph's Boston may be fairly acknowledged to be pre-eminent above its fellows even in this county so famed for noble Churches.

The existing Church was evidently built upon the site of a much smaller and inferior edifice, traces of which were discovered in 1851 during the progress of the restorations then carried out. The first portion commenced was the tower, of the foundation of which Stukeley gives the following account. "Anno 1309, 3rd of Edward II. The foundation of Boston steeple on the next Monday after Palm Sunday in that year, was begun to be digged by many miners and so continued until the Midsummer following, at which time they were deeper than the haven five feet, and they found a bed of stone upon a spring of sand and that laid upon a bed of clay, the thickness of which could not be known." The body of the Church, however, was not probably begun until the reign of

Edward III., a period when many of the Churches in this district were re-built either wholly or in part, and from the changes in the style it is probable that the work was not completed until the expiration of 200 years. The nave with its two aisles is good 14th-century Decorated work, but as the building progressed the Perpendicular style was introduced, and in the completion of the tower and elongation of the chancel was wholly used.

Beginning with the exterior, the chief feature of interest on approaching the Church from a distance is the tower with its light and elegant octagonal lantern. This is divided into four stages. The first, reaching as high as the ridge of the nave roof, contains the great west window, and two others on the north and south sides, as well as the west door, which is broad and low in comparison with the edifice. The second stage contains eight windows, two in each of the walls, consisting of two lights, each with pediment and cinque-foiled tracery, and is a most striking feature of the design both externally and internally. The third stage consists of the bell-chamber lighted by four large windows, and at the base of this an external gallery is carried round the tower. The fourth story contains the octangular lantern itself, the base of which is formed by arches turned diagonally over the angles of the tower. The summit is crowned with a lofty parapet of light traceried work and pinnacles, each terminated by a vane.

The next interesting external feature is the south porch, which, like the adjoining tower has a most imposing effect, flanked by buttresses of elaborate design surmounted with crocketed pinnacles. Attached to the porch on the west side is a large chapel of the Decorated period, which was beautifully restored in 1856 through the liberality of citizens of the American Boston and other places in the United States, as a Memorial to Mr. Cotton, formerly Vicar of Boston, and one of the original founders of the State of Massachusetts.

Passing thence along the south-east side, the buttress next the porch is the first noticeable feature,

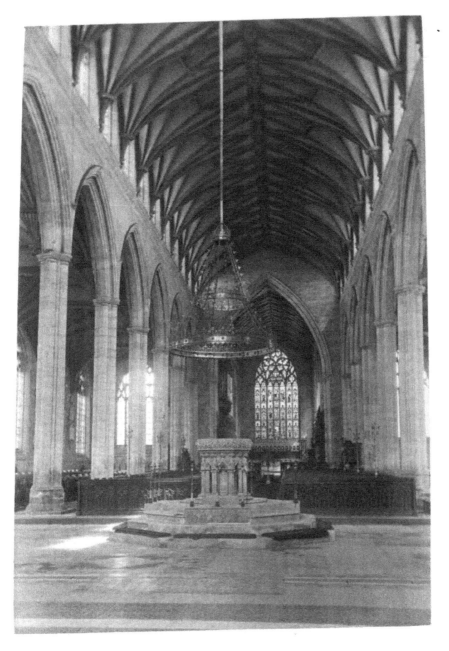

BOSTON.

containing an exquisite niche with crocketed pediment
and canopy and differing in this respect from all the
other buttresses on the south. The south aisle has
five windows of four lights each with Decorated
tracery varying in each window, and between every
window there is a buttress of two stages finishing
with pediments ornamented with masqued gurgoyles.
The east window of the aisle is Perpendicular, and
consists of five lights having cinque-foiled tracery
above. The parapet of the gable is composed of
open quatre-foiled circles. At the angle below is a
buttress of elaborate design having paralleled sides
and niches for figures. Adjoining this, there was until
the last century a two-fold building abutting on the
Church, one portion of which was probably a Chapel
or Oratory and the other was called Taylor's Hall,
but whence its name or what its use does not now
appear.

The chancel is partly Decorated and partly Perpendicular, the three most westward bays being of the
former style and the two eastern of the latter, evi-

c

dently forming an addition to the original design. **On**
each side of the chancel there are five windows, having
four lights in each, except the north-east window, half
of which is blocked up by solid masonry, apparently
with a view to resist the tendency of the walls of
the Church to incline towards the east.

The north aisle in its general details is plainer than
the south. The parapet of its east gable, which is in
late Perpendicular, is of singularly rich and delicate
workmanship, and has been compared to the ornamental work of Henry the Seventh's Chapel at West-
minster.

On entering the Church either through the west
door, or south-west porch, the eye is at once struck
with the vastness of the interior, the whole of which,
being unbroken by transepts or screens, and only inter-
rupted by light arcades, is taken in at one glance.
This, if simply architecturally considered, may be re-
garded as a defect, because it prevents in a great
degree those interchanges of light and shadow on
which so much of the beauty of Gothic buildings

depends : but on the other hand it is an advantage
of more than compensating value when we regard the
requirements of Divine Worship, permitting as it does
vast multitudes to be accommodated within sight
and hearing of the officiating Clergy.   Probably few
buildings of this beauty and magnitude are more
adapted to the Services of the Reformed Church of
England, the whole space, 305 feet in length and (in
the nave) nearly 100 in width, being available more
or less for the use of the worshippers.   Though a
large ante-church is at present unseated, there is
ample accommodation for 2000 persons in the space
allotted for seats ; and some idea may be formed of
the area of the building from the fact that on the
day of the funeral of H.R.H. the Prince Consort, it
was ascertained that 4200 persons were then assembled
within the Church.

The principal features of interest in the interior are
the bold stone vaulting of the tower at the height of
156 feet above the floor, completed during the restoration of 1851 ; the sedilia in the Lady Chapel in the

south-west aisle, and two alabaster altar tombs containing recumbent effigies, the one of a Knight (probably of Malta,) and the other of a lady supposed (though uncertainly) to be Dame Maud or Margery Tylney, the builder of the tower. The ancient stalls in the chancel, 77 in number, have been recently fitted with canopies of elaborately carved oak, and are a feature of great beauty. The east end of the chancel is still in an unfinished state and needs considerable additions, such as a reredos, panelling, etc. Four very richly carved oak sedilia have, however, been lately erected as an instalment towards the work, and steps will probably shortly be taken for the completion of the whole.

The great defect in the interior is the loss of the ancient roof and the substitution of a meaner one 22 feet below the original pitch, which has the effect of destroying the beauty of the clere-story, and gives a depressed appearance to the nave. The wooden roofs of the aisles are of a still more debased type.

It would be impossible in the compass of a brief sketch like the present to give any complete description of this noble Church, and we must be content with indicating (as has now been done) the most prominent points of interest in it. To those who are desirous of more minute information it is needless to say that there are works which treat the subject scientifically and in detail. The above account has been chiefly compiled from Thompson's History of Boston, and the description of the Churches of the Division of Holland, published in 1843.

G. B. BLENKIN.

D

SPALDING, LINCOLNSHIRE.

PALDING parochial Church, dedicated to
GOD in the names of S. Mary and S.
Nicholas, was built by the principal parish-
ioners of the town under the auspices and by the aid
of William Littleport, the Prior of the then flourishing
Monastery of Spalding, A.D. 1284.

This Church was originally Early English in style
of Architecture, and was of the severest character consistent with the sacred purposes for which it
was consecrated. The Early English style had almost
died out at this period ; but life lingers long in
lowland levels.

SPALDING.

Plan. The plan was cruciform ; the nave and transepts having aisles on both sides. The dimensions of the early Church are still defined externally by the original buttresses at the west end of the nave, the north and south ends of the transepts, the south-east buttress of the nave, the south wall of the chancel (which was evidently re-built about this period, upon still visible earlier foundations), and the angle buttresses of the east end of the chancel. This is all that remains externally of the Early English Church. It is more than probable that a cemetery Chapel existed on the site of the present chancel prior to the erection of Littleport's Church ; for the Charters of the Saxon King Bertulph, A.D. 850, speak of two Churches in Spalding : " Lignea Capella Stæ. Mariæ, Anglice Stokyn" on one side of the river, and " Cemeterium Lapidæ Capellæ Scti. Nicholi Anglice Stonyn" on the other side ; and recently, foundations of an early building were discovered, beneath the level of the present floor of the Nave, extending westward from the chancel to midway of the great arches of the transepts.

The line of these foundations was at right angles with the east wall of the chancel, which is nearly two feet out of the square with the present chancel walls, and and is much ruder in masonry. These foundations and the lower courses of the east wall of the chancel formed portions of some ancient Chapel, and may account for the double dedication. If the Early English Church ever had a tower it stood most probably at the west end of the north aisle; for the foundations at that corner were on examination found to be calculated to carry a much greater weight than the rest of the foundations; and that an Early English tower existed somewhere is supposed from the fact of finding Early English base-mouldings and windows re-used and worked into the present tower, which is also largely composed of sepulchral ledger stones of Perpendicular date and some whole coffins. The original clere-stories of the nave and transepts (the latter still existing though not visible externally), were all on the same level, and the roofs would be mitred together at the point of junction. There was no

SPALDING.

tower at the intersection : the angle-piers being carried up, from the foundation to the plate, without either base moulding or capital, as may still be traced, the quoins being visible in the walling. The windows were lancet headed, except the clere-story range of the nave and transepts, which were circular with deeply splayed jambs and sills internally.

The present Church consists of the chancel, with a north Chapel added A.D. 1866 in the Decorated style ; the nave with *two* Perpendicular aisles on each side ; the transepts, (the arcades and clere-stories of which retain their original elevation and features un-altered,) with their eastern aisles, the roofs and walls of which have been raised to admit large and singularly elegant Perpendicular windows ; a Chapel dedicated to S. Thomas of Canterbury having been added to the southernmost bay of the east side of the south transept, A.D. 1315. A Perpendicular tower surmounted by lofty pinnacles with flying buttresses connecting them with a crocketed spire rising to the height of 153 feet from the ground line occupies

E

the western bay of the south outer aisle. A south porch re-built in 1867 ; and a north porch of peculiarly good design and construction, c. 1480, with a groined roof of fan tracery and a parvise over it.

South-west elevation. Viewed externally from the south-west this Church presents an imposing mass of buildings. The expansive elevation of the west front of Perpendicular architecture overbuilt upon and about the sturdy Early English buttresses, with the large seven-light west window rising well into the lofty gable of the nave ; the well proportioned tower, with its " King of Spires" rising royally in the foreground ; with the roof and clere-story range of the nave forming a noble back ground far above and beyond the south porch and aisles, the width of which are indicated by the perspective line of the eave of the transept, the south end of which still retains its early features in one buttress and the triplet lancet window which has been shortened and re-set to bring it within the gable which was flattened when the pitch of the roof was lowered ; and the Chapel of S. Thomas, à Becket, with its peculiar windows of German tracery; and the ridge of the roof of the chancel just visible beyond; its gable cross defining the full extent of the fabric eastwards, completes a picture which when doubled gives some promise of an interior to which it is an introduction.

North-east elevation. Viewed from the north-east the pile of building is equally varied and imposing. In the centre rises the vast nave with its clere-story and embattled parapet in perspective, and its unusual five-light and traceried east window, and gable surmounted by the sancte-bell cot, and flanked at the north-east angle by the octagon stone capped rood-stair turret. On the north side is the transept much altered from its original proportion by lowering its main roof and raising the roof and wall of its eastern aisle, so as to obscure from external view its existing clere-story range and admit the very elegant traceried three-light Perpendicular window. The newly added Chapel or chancel aisle with its flamboyant four-light Decorated east window contrasting strongly with the Early English

triplet window of the chancel east end which has been
(1866) re-built from the string-course below the window
sill. This gable and roof have been recently restored
to their original pitch. On the south side, but not
adjoining the chancel, stands the Chapel of S. Thomas
with its quaint foreign looking traceried window ; the
gable, deprived of its cross possibly when the Chapel
was despoiled by the Crown at the Dissolution in
1535 ; (or in 1539 when by order of the state " the
Abbey was pulled down and sold at 5s. a cart-load,"
and according to the taste of the period " The Parish
Church was much beautified ; ") and not restored when
the building was converted into a Grammar School
by Mr. John Gamlyn, A.D. 1588. In the rear and
above all the numerous roofs and gables rises majes-
tically the grand old spire completing the pyramidical
form of the group.

The interior. Entering the Church by the south
door a forest of pillars stand before us, among which
it is most difficult to discover the plan of the building, until we advance to the nave where, standing at

SPALDING.

the west end, we can survey the vast and lofty space, with two broad aisles on each side, and the transepts with their eastern aisles, and numerous arcades, of which those on each side of the nave are the most lofty. From this spot the whole extent of the Church and Chancel is displayed : a spacious nave of seven arches on each side, its roof is of moulded oak framed together, the hammer beam ends being richly ornamented with carved oak angels with elevated wings and bearing shields with the emblems of the Passion of our Blessed Lord, and other devices. At the east end of the nave above the lofty chancel arch is a five-light window ; and the west end immediately over the door-way is entirely occupied by a magnificent cross window : both these windows have been recently (A.D. 1867) filled most artistically with stained glass in memory of the late Prebendary William Moore, D.D., to whom also the east window of the chancel was presented A.D. 1865. It was towards the close of his long incumbency that the perfect restoration of this glorious Church was initiated.

F

The mode of transforming an Early English into a Perpendicular Church is here singularly exemplified. Originally the nave and transepts were of one uniform height throughout as were also the roofs, plates, clerestory ranges, arches, capitals and bases respectively. The pillars of the nave have been elongated about 6 feet, and the arches re-set when the present clerestory of the nave was substituted for the original (circa. 1450).

Throughout the Church the pillars are four clustered with moulded caps and bases.

A portion of the rood-screen remains soliciting restoration.

The stained glass is all modern but very good. The Church is fitted throughout with open seats for 1200 worshippers. The pulpit is in oak, exquisitely carved, as are also the altar rails and the table which supports the stone altar. On the altar are two appropriate candlesticks, brazen vases, and an altar cross. The chancel is arranged with open stalls on each side. The lectern is a well modelled brass eagle. There are six bells, the earliest is inscribed James Wilesby, C.H. W.D. 1648; the latest, Maurice Johnson, Minister, 1801. The Church has been judiciously restored by G. G. Scott, Esq., at a cost of £ 10,000 and the resident members of the Church both feel and appreciate the blessing thus conferred upon them by Benefactors whose memory lives in their hearts, and for whom may they never cease to pray.

EDWARD MOORE.

SUTTON S. MARY, LINCOLNSHIRE.

YOU have here a Church within a Church, stone of Norman cutting in a Gothic casket ; stone alike and casket being beautiful. Viewed from the exterior, you seem to have before you pointed work almost exclusively* : even this however by no means uniform in date. Sutton Church is a remarkable example of architectural developement. The chancel, the octagon attached to it, the western door, the jambs

---

* On the west wall of the nave there are two Norman buttresses, but they are so unobtrusive, that you have to look close to observe them.

SUTTON.

and head of the western window, and the two western bays of the south aisle are of the Decorated
period : the aisles, one of which is slightly earlier in
date than the other, are Perpendicular : while the south
porch belongs to the Tudor time. It would have been
well if the example of the Gedney clere-story had
fired the monastic residents at Sutton to rival it by a
new clere-story here. But it was reserved for the
stucco period, so the less said about the result the
better.

Such is the casket, the outward Church ; a large
and beautiful specimen of varied- pointed architecture,
with considerable dignity of mass, depth of shadow,
and bold projection. You enter. Of course it is
impossible that the elaborate ranges of Perpendicular
windows, the long and spacious aisles, stretching deep
on either side along the walling of the chancel, should
not tell within, as they tell without. But what surprises
you, is how little they tell ; how they retire back, as
if to hide themselves behind something more massive
and powerful than themselves. You find yourself in

G

a noble Norman nave. On round or polygonal piers ranges of circular arches bear on either side a Norman clere-story. You can trace in either aisle the beautiful blind arcade, through which the windows of the clere-story are pierced at intervals, and see below it the long string course, whence narrow Norman aisles, long since removed, let fall their steeper roof, at the time when that arcade faced the open weather. Of those Norman aisles, the Norman chancel, and its daughter aisles only a few fragments of rubbish remain. The Norman clere-story has become a triforium to the later clere-story that surmounts it. But the nave remains ; and the presence of those massive columns and their plain round-headed arches makes the nave like that of a little Cathedral, while the pointed work of the aisles seems to gain a vigour and firmness, greater than their own, from the association.

Between the early Norman Church and the more spacious building, which partly superseded and partly formed itself upon it, we have a connecting link in the tower. Few districts, probably, can boast so many

beautiful examples of Early English towers, as the
Fen and Marshland. The tower of Sutton S. Mary
is not so delicate in its execution as some of the
others, but it is on a larger scale, and alone retains
the wooden spire and pinnacles, with which it was
originally crowned. The composition of the bell-chamber story is full of grave and simple dignity; and
the double arrangement of the lancets, a triple over-
laid by a double series, almost unique. When it
stood utterly detached from the Norman Church, seen
from base to summit on every face, rearing itself on
its four Early English arches, it must have been singularly majestic. And even since the wide stretch of
the Perpendicular aisle has joined nave and spire to
one another, the point of contact is so slight, that its
solitude is scarcely destroyed.

Among the minor objects of interest, far the most
singular is the octagonal building, with its upper
chamber, at the north-east angle of the Church. It
was designed for the use to which it is at present
applied, and is called a Vestiarium, in a document

dated 1411 A.D. The doorway and short passage connecting it with the north aisle have been recently made : the original access from the Church being the easternmost of the two doorways within the sanctuary. The font is the Norman font, which received the first baptisms ; but it has been much spoiled by re-working. Near it is the slab of an altar, mounted on a wooden frame, and used at present as a table. The aulmry of the Holy Trinity altar remains in the north chancel aisle ; and the piscina of another altar in the south aisle. A good specimen of a latten eagle lectern stands at the entrance of the chancel, and in front of it is a curious leger slab in the pavement, bearing the design of a Calvary cross, and the words " Jesu, mercy," running across the head, " Lady help " across the base. Of the stained glass, nothing remains in the lower lights but a single figure of a knight, with a dragon coiled round his heel, popularly called John of Gaunt, but probably S. George. The little shield above it contains the arms of England, as assumed by Edward the Third, and borne by his successor. The designs

SUTTON.

in the tracery of the windows of the north aisle have
been fairly preserved, especially some beautiful yellows
in the foliage, and care should be taken to work from
what is left, whenever the stained glass in this aisle is
restored. Considerable sums were spent on the Church
in the years 1865-7. The chancel stalls, roof, walls,
and pavement have been thoroughly restored. The
Church fittings have been re-arranged with oak benches.
But there are several minor points connected with the
fabric, which could be restored at small expense, and
should speedily be undertaken : nor should the parish
rest content, until the porches, the tower, the roofs, and
clere-story are rendered worthy of the Church.

The history of the foundation of Sutton Church may
be shortly indicated, by way of commentary on a
deed, dated circa 1180 A.D., by which the site was
granted to the monastery of Castle Acre for that purpose.

The following is a translation :—

" Know all men present and to come, that I William
son of Erneis, by the permission of Nicholaa my wife,

H

give and grant and by this my charter confirm to God
and Saint Mary of Acre, and the monks there serving
God three acres in Sutton in the field, which is called
the old fen land, near a road, to build a Parish
Church, as a free and perpetual gift for the salvation
of my soul, and of Nicholaa my wife, and for the soul
of my father, Robert, son of Erneis, and the soul of my
mother, and for the souls of all my ancestors, and for
the soul of Richard de Haia, and for the souls of all
his ancestors. And I desire that the previous wooden
Church of the same town, as soon as the new Church
is built, be taken away, and the bodies there buried
be carried into the cemetery of the new Church and
there buried, the old cemetery being utterly destroyed.
Witnesses : John the Chaplain, Doun Bardolf, Radulf
Travers, Joichlen de Englebi, Robert de Martinville,
Clarenbald de Merlei, Radulf de Broil, Radulf de
Land, Hugo Bardolf de Putoth, Hugo Angevine,
W. Gernum, William Mackerel, Simon son of Wido,
William Clerk of Dunham, Alestan, Geoffrey Fridai,
and others."

Some sixty years previous to the grant of this land, Robert de Haia, grandfather of Nicholaa, mentioned in this deed, had come into possession of the Manor of Sutton, in right of Muriel, his wife, and had built, on some spot now unknown, a wooden Church. The bodies of two generations had been laid in the church-yard around it, and now William son of Erneis, who has married the heiress, Nicholaa, grants three acres on a different spot, in what is called the old fen land, close to the road, ordering at the same time the bodies to be transferred to the present churchyard, and the old churchyard to be entirely destroyed. We shall probably not be wrong in believing that Nicholaa de Haia had a considerable share in the accomplishment of this grant; and to no one more than to her do we owe the splendour of our Church. She lived to a good old age, was twice married, and had a long widowhood, playing a prominent part in the troubles of King John's reign, and gaining in the course of her life considerable accessions of property in other places. Yet her affection for Sutton Church was con-

stant. From the gifts of her married life sprang the
Norman Church : from those of her widowhood, the
Early English tower : and the large estate bestowed
on the Prior in Sutton, either by herself or her tenants
at her instance and example, formed a treasury, which
must have largely aided the building of the aisles and
porches, which she never saw. In the after history of
the Church no point can be seized with certainty.
Whether the Earl of Salisbury, or the Earls of Lincoln
and Lancaster, who became in turn the possessors of
the Manor, contributed to the enrichment of the Church,
is unknown. By marriage with Blanche of Lancaster,
John of Gaunt became the next possessor of the Sutton
Manor, and it is possible, that the great re-construction
of the Church in the Perpendicular period may be
connected with his gifts while living, or his memory
after death. In the Guild of S. Thomas of Canterbury,
founded in the reign of Henry the Fourth, which had
its Chapel in this Church, masses were said for the
soul of Henry the Fourth and his Queen and John
of Gaunt, until the Reformation. In 1492, the will of

Robert Phillips seems to speak of Church works as then going on, and bequeaths money for their continuance in the sixteen years following. Among those works we may fairly place an alteration of the chancel, by which the Norman chancel arch was raised to its present height, and the chancel aisles opened in a similar way by the erection of lighter, loftier, but very mean arches.

Stukeley, writing in 1724, speaks of the brick clerestory, as erected within the memory of living men. Its flat panelled roof, according with the black oak reredos, now used as an organ screen, was removed some twenty years ago. The eastern windows were inserted at the same time. But the tracery of the west window, and the north-west window, which seems by the same hand, was inserted some sixty years since. The recent works of restoration were executed from the designs of Messrs. Slater and Carpenter.

H. L. BENNETT.

I

GEDNEY, LINCOLNSHIRE.

H E Church of S. Mary, Gedney, is one of the handsomest in the neighbourhood. It consists of a square tower at the west end, about 90 feet high, with a nave 96 feet long, a chancel 48 feet long, and north and south aisles corresponding with the nave in length. The breadth of the Church including these aisles is 65 feet. A handsome south porch of Perpendicular character having on the inner door a Latin inscription (Pax Christi sit huic domui et omnibus habitantibus in eâ, hic requies nostra) forms the principal entrance, and attached to the chancel is a vestry.

GEDNEY.

A small door in the north-west corner of the porch gives access to a turret containing a staircase, leading to a chamber over the porch and still further on to the roof of the Church. The chamber has three windows, south, east, and west. Beneath the east window the ancient altar stone remains, and there is a piscina close by.

A portion of the tower, of the 13th century, is the most ancient part of the structure. It is pierced with lancet windows enriched with shafts and dog-tooth mouldings. The upper story was probably added when the body of the Church was re-built sometime during the 15th century. The whole is terminated by a short conical spire.

In looking at the tower from within the Church, it is evident that three roofs have abutted upon it. The string-course of the original Early English Church remains, above that are indications of a second roof, and the present roof is raised still higher and as a natural consequence is now of very lofty proportion.

The nave contains six arches on each side, and these are surmounted by a clere-story with twelve large Perpendicular windows placed so close together as to give a very light and pleasing appearance to the Church. The roof, which is the original of the Perpendicular period, though in some parts roughly mended, makes an appropriate finish to the whole.

The chancel is very handsome. It is divided from the nave by a carved oak screen under the chancel arch, and is furnished with oak stalls. A rather flat roof was removed a few years ago, and an ornamental one, at the original pitch, added by the Ecclesiastical Commissioners, who are the owners of the Rectorial property.

G. ROGERS.

MOULTON.

MOULTON, LINCOLNSHIRE.

THE Church at Moulton * dedicated to All
Saints is one of those large fabrics for
which the County of Lincoln is so noted,
and although there may be others of greater interest
yet this Church should by no means be passed by.

The tower at the west end with its crocketed
spire is undoubtedly the most striking feature, especially when approached from either the north-west or
south-west, but perhaps the view from the north-east

---

* For this notice we are indebted to William Smith, Esq., Architect, London,
who has just completed the restoration of this Church. (Ed.)

K

corner of the churchyard—with the pinnacled east gable—the long line of arcaded clere-story to the nave—and the tower and spire at the west rising high above all—gives the best idea of the great size of the building that can be obtained.

On reference to the plan, the Church will be seen to consist of a nave with north and south aisles, by 94 feet long by 59 feet wide. Chancel 45 feet 20 feet. Western tower 15 feet square—all inside dimensions. The extreme external length being 171 feet. A vestry and organ chamber on the north side of chancel and a new south porch have been added during the alterations carried out last year.

In almost all our old parish Churches we find the work of many different periods and this Church is no exception to the general rule. The earliest portion now existing is the nave. Here the arches separating the nave from the aisles and the walls over them, and the arcaded clere-story are Early English, probably erected at the commencement of the 13th century.

This early nave had originally narrower aisles about 10 feet wide, but these were taken down and replaced by the present wider aisles in the 14th century.

On the south side some of the early buttresses still exist, but not in their original position.

Next in order comes the fine tower and spire rising to a height of about 160 feet. This work appears to have been erected about the date 1400 and apparently immediately after its completion the chancel was taken in hand and entirely re-built, as there is scarcely a vestige of early work left in the present chancel. A handsome rood screen was placed at the chancel-arch with overhanging rood loft. This in later times has been terribly mutilated and the original overhanging gallery has been removed. The stone staircase to the rood loft, however, still remains in the angle of the chancel and south aisle. In the north wall of the chancel, within the sacrarium, there was a richly carved, and triple canopied tomb, but almost every trace of ornamental work has been utterly destroyed. On the north side of the chancel, a vestry with a chamber over it for the priest, was erected, but this, too, has been taken down.

The beautiful early arcaded clere-story with every 3rd arch pierced, which had hitherto escaped alteration, was spoiled by the insertion of the present large windows, one of which now occupies the space of two of the original arches. Probably this alteration was made when the high pitched roof of the nave was taken away and the present one substituted.

In still later times the tracery of all the side and east windows of the aisles was entirely removed, hideous pews and a western gallery were allowed to block up the interior, and a vestry was formed by entirely enclosing the western bay of the north aisle. These were swept away in 1867, and the Church brought back to more seemly condition.

In "Lincolnshire Churches" published in 1842 there is a quotation to the effect that "Col. Holles" took notes of sundry remains of stained glass, but not a fragment remained when the recent works were undertaken ; and here it may be stated that on clearing

MOULTON.

out the old pews, &c., no encaustic tiles or carving of any kind was found. Part of the base of a Perpendicular font with a few other moulded stones and a small piece of framing of some seats of the same date were all that could be discovered.

On entering the Church by the south door one cannot but be struck with the general massiveness of the columns of the nave. They are mostly formed by clustered shafts and have carved capitals. The old bench table or seat round the bases may still be seen.

The Photograph will give a good idea of the general view looking west, with the lofty tower-arch, the groined ceiling, and good west window.

On reference to the plan and photograph the columns at *A* will be noticed as quite different to any of the others. There is every reason to believe that originally an arch was thrown across the nave at this point, but for what object is not so certain.

It has been conjectured that the western bay of the present nave formed originally the lower story of

L

a tower, but against this theory there are several objections which it seems difficult to reconcile.

That there was a campanile of some sort to the early Church is quite evident as the Rev. E. Moore mentions a record that " in 1292, Bishop Sutton, holding a Court at Croyland, ordered the people of Moulton not to hold fairs and markets in the church-yard but rather to set about repairing their campanile."

It is possible that this "campanile" may have been merely a bell gable carried on the cross arch just mentioned and pierced for two or three bells after the manner of other existing examples of the kind ; and that as it was found defective in construction, bell gable and arch under were entirely cleared away.

The position certainly is unusual, but we have the pretty nearly positive evidence that an arch was thrown across the nave at this point for some purpose. One thing is quite certain that when the present tower was built, the high pitched roof existed on the nave quite to the west wall, and that the present tower was built against it. This may be clearly seen by the stone weathering now existing on the east face of the tower.

The neighbouring Early Churches both of Whaplode and Weston have no Early western towers.

The western face of the tower is still very handsome as may be seen by the Photograph, but the general effect is much marred by the loss of the sculpture which originally filled the now empty niches.

There is a curious arrangement for sedilia and piscina in one of the window sills of the south aisle. There is also a piscina near the east end of south aisle and one in the eastern respond of the north aisle arcade, shewing that altars once existed there.

In the pavement at the west end of north aisle there is a stone slab with incised cross and chalice, and the matrix of some small brasses, but no old brasses are to be found in the Church. There are also two other stones with a cross incised in one and a chalice in the other.

On the tower piers two old "masons' marks" may be seen.

HOLBEACH, LINCOLNSHIRE.

OLBEACH Church is the most perfect example of the Decorated period of architecture in that unrivalled series of Churches extending form Boston to Lynn, viâ Spalding. It is the laudable ambition of the present day to restore such of these Churches as have survived the scathing process of a Reformation : that tender process which left only one place of worship for the pure and reformed religion in this vast parish, more than 20 miles long. The attempt is being made, not unsuccessfully, to restore this Church, and Churches to this parish, and the people to the Church.

The Church is dedicated to the service of GOD in the name of All Saints, and consists of a nave of seven

HOLBEACH.

bays with a range of fourteen two-light clere-story windows on each side : north and south aisles uniform in
length with the nave and more than 18 feet wide : a
chancel ample and lofty, a substantial spire-capped tower
at the west end of the nave and as wide ; north and
south porches and a canopied west entrance. Externally,
the Church has a very attractive appearance. It is large
and lofty, and its parts—chancel, nave, aisles, tower, and
spire—well proportioned. The tracery of the chancel
and aisle windows being of the easy flowing character
of the early part of the reign of K. Edwd. III.
(circa 1340). The clere-story, tower, and spire are a
few years later, probably of the reign of K. Rich. II.
(circa 1380). Notwithstanding this difference in the
date of the respective parts, there is such uniformity
in construction that it is very probable there was no
material departure from the original design, merely an
interruption in the progress of the work. The earliest
mention of a Church in Holbeach, so far as I know at
present, is that "in the year 1189 Thomas de Multon
having with almost all the most powerful men of the

M

Wapentake of Elloe conspired against the Abbot of
Croyland, tumultuously assembled sometimes in a barn
at Weston belonging to the Prior of Spalding, and
sometimes in the Church at Holbeach." The only visible trace remaining of the Church of this date, on the
the site of this Church may be the Norman capital
which lies on the floor at the south-east corner in the
nave, and some few of the very numerous corbel heads
at the terminations of the hood moulds of the clere-
story windows, which are grotesque and rude enough to
have been the production of a Norman workman.

According to Marrot the sancte bell was presented
to the Church A.D. 1453, by W. Enot, of Lynn, and
Henry Neale, of Holbeach ; it would hang in the
bell-cot on the east gable of the nave, where the naked
looking stone arch now stands with the date of 1629
upon it : a mere skeleton of the original, but even
this is a great improvement on the decapitated gables
of some neighbouring Churches. A curious lot of
articles were sold by the Churchwardens of Holbeach
according to K. Henry VIII's. injunction, 1547, from

which we may gather that there were several altars in this Church, namely, the Holy Trinity, S. Nicolas, S. James, Our Lady of Pity, S. Thomas of Canterbury, besides the high altar, and many ornaments and vestments of much interest. The Church at that time was well furnished with painted windows which it now needs very much, especially in the chancel. From that time, till within the last few years, I should conceive everything that was done to this Church, whether with good or bad intentions, tended to its mutilation. Its present state is very creditable to its guardians who are working with a will to repair the injuries of past generations.

Notwithstanding the urgent want of a vestry, I doubt if they will have the boldness to re-erect the convenient little sacristy which was taken down A.D. 1567, soon after it was erected, on the south side of the chancel, eastward of the priest's door.

It is difficult to obtain a satisfactory view of this Church, the cemetery around it is so crowded with trees and huge head stones, very few of which have

either form or execution to recommend them. One to
the late learned Vicar, the Rev. James Morton, is a
good exception. Standing so as to see the north-east
view of the Church the whole pile is very grand.
The principal feature is the very massive tower 86 feet
high, carrying by far the largest spire in Holland, said
to be 100 feet high. The proportions of the tower and
spire, and the skilful manner in which the one is adapted to the other are most admirable ; and the execution of the work, especially of the spire with its six,
teen spire-lights, gabled, hooded, and corbled, with the
plain bold roll at its angles supported at each of its four
corners by a stone crozier, is very masterly, and properly
ranks among the best examples of the earliest Perpendicular period. The embattled parapet of this tower is
very effective, though now robbed of its angle pinnacles.

The clere-story range from this point of view is very
pleasing. The fourteen two-light windows are divided
into pairs by buttresses of three stages each : these
buttresses originally rose above the embattled parapet
and each carried a pinnacle : if these could be restored

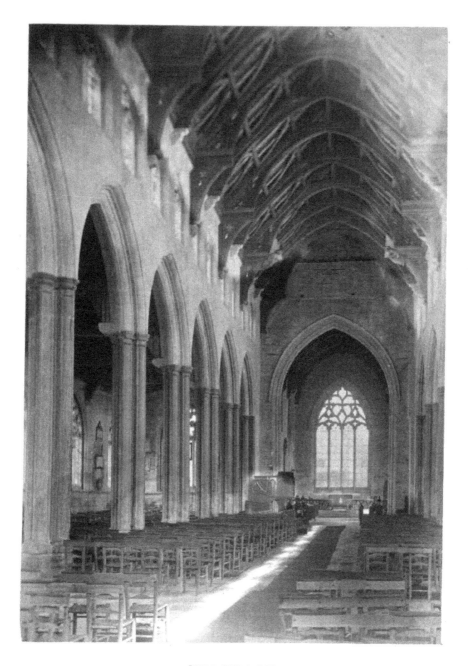

HOLBEACH.

the elevation would be much improved : even the stack pipes, alternating with the buttresses, in this range are made to add to the effect. Very few clere-stories have so much variety, so much light and shade, as is here produced. Throughout, the windows of this Church are very prominent and attractive features. The aisle walls, too, being parapeted and embattled, but low enough not to obscure the clere-story, produce a multiplicity of detail which at once rivets the attention. It is to be regretted that the chancel walls were not parapetted, as I believe they were before the recent alteration by the Ecclesiastical Commission. The main buttresses through-out this Church are uniformly good, terminating with gable tops and a trefoiled ridge mould. Those of the chancel have elegant engaged tracery within the gables, and those of the tower carried each either a cross or a crocket. The north porch is no part of the original building and contrasts very strangely with the Church. It is considerably later in date and has so much the appearance of a baronial gate house that I am inclined to think it was never designed for an ecclesiastical

N

porch, and very probably, like the turret stairs on the south side of Spalding Church, has been removed from its original site and set up in its present position. The base moulds are very cleverly adapted to the base moulds of the aisles; but not more cleverly than the base moulds of the chancel, which can only be detected on close inspection as of later date than the aisle base moulds. The porch is flanked at the north-east and north-west angles by massive circular towers, one being a stone stair turret leading to the parvise and roof, and the other a groined cell or porter's lodge. The windows of the parvise, being deprived of their mullions, are ugly; and the upper part of one of the towers, having been inartistically re-built, looks crippled and bad. On examining the steps, some of which have 14 inches rise, I think it is pretty clear this porch has been in work elsewhere.

The south porch is contemporaneous with the Church and retains its lofty pitch and acutely pointed arch which has not only had tracery in the head but has indications also of having been glazed, the glass grove being still visible. The door within this porch is a beautiful example of Decorated wood tracery, so elaborate yet so simple in setting out. The south doorway has moulded jambs and arch : the bases and caps are also moulded but not of any good design. The north doorway has unfortunately been cleaned and consequently the fillet on the inner moulding is clean gone.

In the west front of the tower is a well recessed doorway flanked on either side with a double buttressed projecting jamb which carries a hood or stone roof carved on the underside in imitation of groining. The roof of this door-porch like the west doorway of S. Margaret, of Lynn, rises into the five-light west window of the tower, which is similar to the windows in the north and south faces of the tower. The tracery in these windows is peculiar and not likely to be much copied.

Entering the Church by this west door we find ourselves under a groined roof, within the ample tower which opens into the nave by a high and massive archway, the jambs and arch of which are boldly moulded.

The Church from this point displays a wide and lofty nave, the seven arcades of which on either side are supported by slender and elegant shafts of four-clustered piers, filleted, with a deep hollow mould in the returning angle. The caps are meanly moulded; the arches are pointed and consist of two members, the two eastern-most of the north arcade and the easternmost on the south arcade having the deep hollow mould in the returning angle of the piers continued between the members of the arch. The windows of the aisles at the east end are also more elaborately moulded than the rest of the windows. The east ends of the aisles have been no doubt important chapels, and intended so to be originally, and it is more than probable that some illus-trious families appropriated to their own use for prayer and sepulture these portions of the Church in con-sideration of their being great benefactors to the fabric.

The altar-tomb of Sir Humphrey Littlebury, (born 1346,) was erected originally at the east end of the north aisle, stands now at the west end of this aisle. It is a rich altar tomb with four canopied niches on each side, richly carved and diapered with roses, and eight shields repeating the coat of Littlebury, *ar.* 2 *lions passant guardant gu.* alternately with *Kirton gu.* 3 *bars erm.* Upon this tomb is the recumbent effigy of a knight in armour of the costume of 1388, his hands conjoined and raised in prayer, on his arm his shield, his head resting on his crest (a head in a close fitting net), his feet supported on a lion. This beautiful monument, once doubtless gorgeous in colour, has been recklessly cleaned and every bit of colour removed, in fact literally flayed. In the north wall is an arched recess made doubtless to receive the tomb of one of the benefactors of the Church. And in the south wall the third bay from the east has been cleverly re-built: the window inserted in this bay is a miserable imitation of the other aisle windows. Possibly there may have been a Chapel projected here and destroyed at the Reformation.

The stone rood-stairs in the south-east angle of the nave, entered from the south aisle, so cleverly inserted in the respond, are no part of the original building.

o

The roof of the nave, which until last year was of unwrought timbers, has been most substantially replaced by a well constructed and thoroughly ecclesiastical and appropriate hammer-beam roof. The angels are too corporeal : they appear rather to weight than to carry the roof.

The chancel was re-built very soon after the building of the Church : the windows are unusually large, and the whole of the view of the interior of this beautiful Church is very much marred by having a four-light instead of a three or five-light window over the altar. Fortunately the tracery is very good. All the window arches as well as the main arch of the chancel have hood mouldings. A string course and hoods in the nave would have added materially to the architectural picture of the interior.

The length of the Church is 168 feet, and the width 68 feet.

EDWARD MOORE.

WESTON.

WESTON, LINCOLNSHIRE.

TH E Church of S. Mary the Blessed Virgin at Weston, three miles north of Spalding, was until recently comparatively unknown, though owing to the process of exhuming and reparation, which was diligently applied to it by the late Vicar, it now deservedly ranks among the best models in England for a village Church.

The Nave of five bays, together with the clere-story and the south porch are Early English or Transition (circa 1160) of the best type. The Chancel of three bays Lancet (possibly re-built circa 1280). North and south Transepts (added circa 1350 and 1360)

Decorated. The south Aisle and the north Aisle suc-
cessively re-built (circa 1380) and the Tower at the west
end of the nave (circa 1400) Perpendicular though not
vertical : for unfortunately the foundations of the tower
and other parts of the Church have yielded irregularly
and the whole fabric looks, as has been said, as if
some monster had got under it and upheaved it.

An earlier Church than any part of the present one
must have existed here, for in the reign of K. Henry I.
(circa 1135), Thomas de Multon, when attending the
funeral of his father in the Abbey of Spalding, gave
to the monks of that house, in the presence of their
Chapter and of the members of his family, the Church
of Weston, of which he was the patron. The gift was
conveyed by the act of depositing his clasped knife on
the altar of the Abbey. This Thomas de Multon was
father to Lambert, whose marble tomb Colonel Holles
records as being in the north choir. There is now, in
the north-east corner of the north transept, a much
perished sepulchral slab, which had the lined effigies of
a man and woman indented on its surface, with just

sufficient of the inscription left to identify it as the tomb of Lambert and Matilda his wife. The arms emblazoned in the window over, *argent two bars gules*, proclaimed him a de Moulton. He doubtless, like his relatives of Holbeach and Moulton, by being a bene-factor to the Church, acquired the honour of sepulture within its walls.

Near to this slab, and raised about one foot from the ground to protect it from desecration, is the origi-nal altar-stone of the Church. The consecration crosses at the corners are still visible. The stone, though very thick and naturally tough, is broken diagonally across, and rejointed, whereby its length has been shortened, yet it still serves for a standard by which other origi-nal altar-stones may be challenged. Nearly in front of this is the sepulchral slab of the Rev. Willyam Whettaker, "A reverend minister of God's Word in this parish," who, dying in 1640, dare hardly be called Vicar. On the west wall of this transept is a tablet to the Rev. John Morton, Vicar, who in 1720 was the last resident Vicar in Weston until 1866. Mr. Morton, by his Will left

P

£20 to the poor of the parish, and a suit of black for the covering of the altar on Good Friday.

The Chancel, presents, externally, a very pleasing and ecclesiastical design : three bays on each side separated by slightly projecting buttresses of two stages each : in each bay a tall lancet window, perfectly plain : on the south side, in the westernmost bay, there is, under the window, an earlier circular headed priest's door-way, and westward of it, there is, thrust in, a tall square headed, two-light, low-side window, the vertical iron bars of which, as usual, do not come in contact with the sill. A continuous horizontal string course immediately below the window sills, and banding the buttresses, divides the elevation into two stages. A notch-head water table extends along the nave, and the walls carry a high pitched roof, covered with lead, as were almost all the Holland Churches, until recent restorations have obliterated this and other interesting characteristic features in several instances. The east end of this chancel is well worthy of imitation. There are three lofty lancet headed windows, set between four buttresses, which rise to an equal height with the window-heads which range, almost in a line, with the springers of the high pitched gable, in which is a very elegant quatrefoil window : the whole is surmounted with a well proportioned English cross.

The south clere-story of the nave consisted of a row of, originally, five single-light, round headed windows, with double engaged shafts at the jambs, and moulded heads, the two easternmost were altered when the transept was added, and the westernmost is a modern insertion : the water table is notch and corbel head at the same level as the water table of the chancel. The roof of the nave does not rise so high as the chancel. The clere-story windows on the north side are plainer than those on the south, having an uninterrupted bold roll banding the jambs and head of each window.

The south porch is, externally, perfectly plain on the east and west sides. The entrance is a high pointed arch springing from moulded capitals which rest, on either side, on three detached slender columns. Internally this porch is like a little E. E. Chapel : upon the stone bench on each side, and which returns, stopping against the doorway at the entrance to the Church, stand boldly detached columns, with moulded bases and gracefully carved caps, supporting arcades set deeply in the thickness of the walls. It is covered in with a substantial oak and lead roof.

Entering the Church by this doorway, the effect is that of a Cathedral in miniature, but the whole tone of the building is more solemn and suggestive of devotional feeling than many of our Cathedrals. The nave arches are E. E. massive and pointed, the first member has a bold hollow and roll mould, the second has a plainly chamfered edge : these arches rest on ample circular caps, very boldly and elegantly carved. The shafts are short and slender, the south range being octagonal and the north circular, and each pier is surrounded by four disengaged cylindrical slender shafts connected with the base and cap of each. The roof is alternate tie and hammer-beam of the Perpendicular period.

The chancel arch rises from well-carved capitals resting on angular jambs with detached shafts. It is a high pointed arch, very deeply moulded.

The chancel, beyond this, presents an unusually attractive feature. It is arcaded on each side by three plain pointed arches springing from small bell-shaped capitals ornamented with the nail-head mould : these capitals are supported by slender shafts rising from bases standing on the stone benches which run along the walls. The east end has three lancet headed windows set under engaged arches which spring from slender banded columns : over these a quatre-foil gable window. The roof is a tie-beam and post roof, well timbered and appropriate.

Looking towards the west end of the nave, the tower, with its large four-light and transomed Perpendicular window, seen through the ample tower-arch, though not in character with the nave itself, is not unpleasing ; but the good effect is very much impaired, by the inclination of the tower towards the west ; this produces a very singular optical delusion. It is difficult to reconcile to the eye which lines of masonry preserve the true vertical, until tested by the bell ropes which are here suspended from the bell-chamber floor to the

Q

ground, without those ugly and unnecessary sally-balks.

The general effect of this Church is much enhanced by the character of the open benches throughout. None of the wood-work is fixed. The reading desk, lectern, and pulpit are each good in construction and appropriateness, though the first is now wrongly and unnecessarily placed in the nave. The altar is a temporary table, wholly unworthy any Church, much more such a Church. The font is the best in the Deanery by far : the bowl is circular, divided by engaged shafts into eight compartments, each having a stiff foliaged trefoil sprig boldly carved : the date is circa 1180.

EDWARD MOORE.

WHAPLODE.

WHAPLODE, LINCOLNSHIRE.

THIS parochial Church is dedicated to S. Mary. The nave of seven bays is the longest and narrowest in South Holland ; longer than Spalding, and narrower than Cowbit. The five east-ernmost bays and the chancel arch are Norman (circa 1080) ; the three westernmost bays with the west front ; and the tower, which forms the south bay of the south transept ; and the doorway, which has been re-set in the south aisle wall, are Early English (circa 1190). The east end of the chancel, and one bay of its north wall, with the pillar in that wall ; and the jambs of the arch at the east end of the north aisle are Decorated (circa 1320). The north transept and the north and south aisles are Perpendicular, as are also the walls of

the nave above the clere-story windows, and the top
cornice and battlement of the tower, (circa 1420). The
north and south porches ; and the walling up of the
arches in the north wall of the chancel, in the east
end of the north aisle ; and in the north face of the
tower are post-Reformation, (circa 1540). The south
wall of the chancel is unmitigated builder's Gothic of
the enlightened 19th century.

Approaching this village Church on the south side
we are at first struck with amazement at the vast
extent of the nave, with its enlarged and ugly aisles,
with its windows, all but one, denuded of their tracery ;
and the clere-story windows, which have been altered
and each key-stone crutched up by a centre mullion.
Above this deformity rises an elegantly high-pitched and
leaded roof, and still higher pitched gables surmounted by bold crosses of Early English character. Here,
too, is the most glorious Early English tower, standing upon an exceedingly well conceived base, adjoining
the southernmost bay of the south aisle. This tower
consists of four stages ; the lowest stage is arcaded, on

each of its three exposed faces, with five pointed arches, of zigzag mould, rising from tall and slender detached cylindrical shafts : the next stage is also arcaded, but with only three arches, similarly supported as in the lower stage ; the centre arch in three of the faces is occupied by a deeply recessed window : the next stage is similarly treated on all four faces : and the upper stage—the bell-chamber—contains in each face a pair of most beautifully proportioned and elaborately wrought windows ; the centre mullions and tracery have been most barbarously removed, but notwithstanding all the ill-treatment this tower has received, and though capped with a late embattled parapet and ball-headed pinnacles, ill becoming such an exquisitely designed campanile, it is yet "a thing of beauty." In every particular of symmetry, construction, detail, and material this is, by far, the most perfect specimen of architecture in the Deanery of Holland.

The west front of the nave was originally conceived in the same spirit and architectural skill as the tower, but it has been so grievously mutilated it is pitiable

R

to behold. Sufficient, however, is left to enable a competent architect to restore its twelve columns, which support the moulded members of the pointed arch of the doorway, with its niche on either side, and the five-light window above it.

The north side of the Church presents a very stern aspect, and bears unmistakeable tokens of hard usage. The clere-story consists of a range of twenty-six arches, seven of which are pierced for windows. The nebule water-table has been re-built and inverted. The north transept, till recently, has been unscrupulously adapted for the village school room, with such alterations as indicate a period of neglect and desecration which should make us thankful that any portion of the Church has outlived such times.

The chancel has been cut down, re-roofed, and nearly re-built : we regret to say substantially.

The interior of the Church is remarkably massive and bold in structure and decoration. The chancel arch is semicircular and low, but 13 feet in span : it springs from cushioned caps on detruncated engaged shafts : the mouldings on its west front are the double arcade, lozenge, zigzag, and roll: it carries one huge unbroken mass of masonry, on which was once depicted in fresco a representation of some religious subject now entirely obliterated by the colour-wash of the 18th and the scarifying process of the 19th century. The eastern responds, and the first four-and-a-half piers, on each side of the nave, are Norman of a very massive size, with very large abaci, supported on cushioned capitals. These carry Norman semicircular arches. The western responds, with the two next piers-and-a-half on each side of the nave, are Early English. The clerestories over these respective portions of the nave follow the dates of the piers and arches over which they stand, and the bifrons pier, supporting the arches where the two periods of architecture meet, unites the two styles by partaking of both. The nave, though 110 feet long, is only 19 feet wide: the aisles on either side of the nave are each more than 16 feet wide. The area of this Church is so extensive that only the eastern portion of it is fitted with open seats, for the accommodation of the worshippers ; the rest of the Church, forming a sort of ante-Church, is entirely open, which gives it quite a Cathedral appearance.

The nave is covered by a hammer-beam Perpendicular roof ; the principals, collar-beams, and rafters are moulded, and the spandrils filled in with open tracery.

The rood stairs are partly cut into the respond, and partly enclosed in a sort of stone cupboard which stands in the south-east corner of the nave. This is Tudor work.

The chancel is very uninviting, and retains but little of its original, except its ground plan, dimensions, and its decorated east window jambs.

The south wall is perfectly plain, with a three-light domestic window midway : the tympanum of the Norman priest's door is converted into a walling stone near its original position. On the north side are two arches walled up. These, no doubt, opened into a side Chapel, now destroyed.

A simple wooden table has been substituted for the altar which, with almost every destructible relic of interest, appears to have perished at the boasted Reformation.

The font is probably a creditable imitation of the original Norman font, and is well and significantly mounted near the great west entrance.

In the west end of the south aisle is a monument to the Irby family. Under a dome, supported by ten Grecian pillars, lie, on a platform raised about 4 feet from the ground, the full life sized effigies of a knight and his lady, which the inscription around the cornice, as well as the emblazoned coat, *Ar. a fret of 8 pieces sa. on a canton gu. a chaplet or.* show it to be Sir Anthony Irby and his wife. He was the son of Sir Anthony Irby by Alice daughter of Thomas Welbie, Esq., and died 1624.

At the west end of the north aisle lie two stone coffins, with the ledger stones belonging to them. These lay a few inches below the present floor line of the east end of the nave when they were exhumed during the process of re-flooring the Church in 1850. One is a particularly good example of a raised

s

and foliated Early English cross. Each coffin contained a skeleton, with a fragile, soft, metal chalice and paten on the breast.

The five bells were re-cast in 1718: the mottoes do credit to the then vicar. "Laudo Deum verum." "It clamor ad cælos." "Ut mundus sic nos nunc lætitiam nunc dolorem." "Plebem voco congrego clerum." "Defunctos plango vivos moneo."

We are indebted to the REV. EDWARD MOORE, F.A.S., for the above notes, made by him in 1851.

CROYLAND ABBEY.

THIS celebrated Abbey, having experienced the extremes of prosperity and adversity, is now reduced to a comparatively lifeless corpse, or rather the amputated limb only, of its original structure. The spirit has departed. The present Abbey no more resembles what it was in its glory, than the fragments of a vase convey the grace and use of the scent-jar; yet in some measure it retains one quality of the jar which

> "Break as you will,
> The scent of the roses will hang to it still:—"

so of this remnant of the Abbey, ruined and despoiled as it is, the odour of sanctity hovers around it, and the grandeur of architecture, and the venerable tones of antiquity combine with historical recollections to reward the archæological student who may visit the Abbey of Croyland.

The various fabrics which have occupied this site from the time when the Knight Guthlac became the Hermit who first planted his cell on the desolate Island of Croyland, about A.D. 710,—the cell which was re-placed by a Church and Monastery to the honour of God in the name of St. Mary, and endowed by the grateful benefaction of K. Ethelbald, A.D. 716, and built anew A.D. 1061—1085, by Abbot Wulketul: and again more beautifully by Abbot Joffrid, circa, A.D. 1114, have been literally carried away, with the exception of some fragments of the last Abbey erected to the glory of God in honour of St. Guthlac and St. Bartholomew.

The Abbey now consists mainly of the north aisle of the nave with a western tower, and some portions of the nave walls: altogether little more than one fifth of the Abbey itself. This north aisle

has always been used as the parochial Church of
Croyland. It seems to have been originally constructed for a separate purpose from the rest of the Abbey,
as there still remains (at A), in the west front of the
tower (though concealed from view by the accumulated
buttresses on the south side of the porch) the south
jamb, capital and several feet of a large Norman
moulded arch, ornamented with the nail-head and co-
eval with the oldest part of the west front of the
south aisle. These formed the south side of a doorway, at least as wide as the present west door-way
of the nave, and consequently an independent principal
entrance. Moreover, on 4th September, 1292, Bishop
Sutton held a court at Croyland, and in 1486, Bishop
Russell also held a court "in the Parish Church, within the conventual Church, and on the north side" thereof.
It appears to have been so used at the Dissolution, which
accounts for its not being destroyed by the Reformers
with the rest of the Abbey. From the walling up
of the great arch at the east end of the nave and of the
door-ways in the screen we may conclude the nave

T

and south aisle were at the Reformation reserved also for parochial use.

The north aisle 93 feet by 26 feet consists of six bays, with three chapels on the north side attached to the three westernmost bays, and a tower of large proportions at the west end, with a porch for its western entrance. The west wall of the nave, and a portion of the west end of the south aisle, with three of the westernmost of the nine arches of the south arcade of the nave, and the westernmost arch of the great central tower are not yet destroyed.

Inspecting these ruins from the south west, the early work of Abbot Joffrid deserves notice as the oldest part of the Abbey. His west front of the south aisle consists of five stages, all more or less decorated with moulded arcading, carried on slender cylindrical shafts.

A massive Perpendicular buttress divides this Norman work from the grand west front which was most opportunely preserved A.D. 1860, by the combined efforts of the present Rector and the Vicar

of an adjoining parish, with the skill of that most
conservative Architect G. Gilbert Scott, Esq., F.S.A.
This interesting Early English monument of monkish
art consists of an elaborately decorated façade of 70
feet in height. The whole front from the ground to
the summit is covered with more than life-size statues
within rich canopied niches. In the centre is a double
door-way, most elaborately moulded and carved. In
the tympanum is a large quatre-foil containing five
sculptured medallions referring to scenes in the history
of St. Guthlac. The subjects in basso-relievo are
the landing of St. Guthlac: the dedication of his
Church: his driving out the Croyland devils with his
scourge: his burial and his apotheosis. Over the
door-way is a large window; originally an Early
English window or windows occupied the width, but
not the height of the present opening, as may be seen
by the moulded Alwalton marble jambs and carved
capitals still remaining, upon which are stilted the
jambs of the subsequent Perpendicular six-light window
of similar dimensions and tracery as the west window

in the tower by its side. All above the spring of
the window arch is Perpendicular. The statues in
four tiers above the doorway represent (1) the Apostles
(2) Tutelar Saints and Royal Patrons, and on either
side of the window (3 and 4) the benefactors of the
Abbey. On each side of the doorway were beautifully sculptured statues, one only of which now remains.

On the north side of this celebrated west front
stands a massive Perpendicular Tower, originally open
to the nave on the south side, and by a lower
arch on the east face to the aisle, with large windows
on the west, north, and east faces. Its foundations seem to have yielded to its weight, and extra
buttresses of enormous size have been added on its
north side. A porch of late Perpendicular work with
a well lighted parvis over it has been projected from
the west front of the tower. The tower is covered
in with a stone roof in the form of a stunted octagon
spire.

The nave is in ruin. The north arcade consisting
of the great arch of the tower and seven Perpendicular

arches standing on piers whose moulded sides run into the arches uninterrupted by capitals. On the south side were nine similar arches, only three of which remain. Above this arcade ran a passage from end to end in the thickness of the wall, like a triforium; and over this a range of very large clere-story windows; one only now remains and it is walled up against the tower.

At the east end of the nave is the western arch of the Norman central tower: it is lofty and the full width of the nave: only the zig-zag soffit-ring of the arch remains; it springs from angular capitals.

The eastern responds of the Norman arcade and triforium are left in the nave. A small portion of the south west angle of this tower rises over the spiral staircase. On the external face of this piece of masonry may be traced the springer for the groining ribs of the nave and transept aisles; the weathering of their roofs; the jamb and capital and arch of the Norman clere-story both of the nave and transept;

v

and above this the weathering of the roofs of the Norman nave and transept, and the chamfered angle of the central tower which must have been considerably larger than the existing western tower.

Some idea of the stupendous size and elegance of this tower may be formed by passing through the screen and viewing the piers from the east.

The great window thrust into the second arch from the western tower is modern Gothic.

The brickwork which fills in the great arch at the east end of the nave was no doubt built up when the Abbey was destroyed in 1539 reserving the nave and its aisles for parochial use. These were very much injured during the civil war in 1643. In 1688 the wooden roof of the nave fell in, and the arches of the north side were then walled up. Since that time the north aisle only has been used as the parish church and the rest of the Abbey suffered to fall to decay : much of the material has been carried away for repairing roads and banks, and portions have been pulled down to provide material for the walls which

were built when the churchyard was enlarged within
the last 10 years.

Entering by the porch we come into the spacious
and lofty tower in which there are no less than five
stone galleries of various heights in the thickness of
the walls.

The interior of the Abbey is most depressing. A
great ugly gallery occupies more than the westernmost
bay, and under it in gloomy shade stands the massive
Perpendicular font, and in a singular panelled niche on
the south side is a very large Early English font
built into a Perpendicular wall. Over the altar and
occupying nearly two of the easternmost bays is
another hideous gallery like a "grand stand" and in
the east of the Chapels is there an upper story like
opera boxes: the ground floor is divided into substantial closed pews recently improved and gothicised and
a three decker of approved elevation is planted about
midway of the south wall and the seats throughout
are arranged so that the spectators may watch the
minister and those in the galleries may look down

upon him. The roof of the existing aisle is groined of the date of the first quarter of the 15th century, the rebus on the boss of the fourth bay may refer to Abbot Overton or Abbot Litlyngton its builders.

This Abbey and Rectory should be a caution against "sweeping changes," and over zealous "Reformers" who clamour for "disendowment," as well as "disestablishment."

EDWARD MOORE.

END OF THIRD SERIES.

THE

FEN AND MARSHLAND

CHURCHES;

THIRD SERIES.

GROUND PLANS.

For this series of Plans the Editors
are indebted to the
Rev. EDWARD MOORE, M.A., F.S.A.,
Vicar of Spalding.

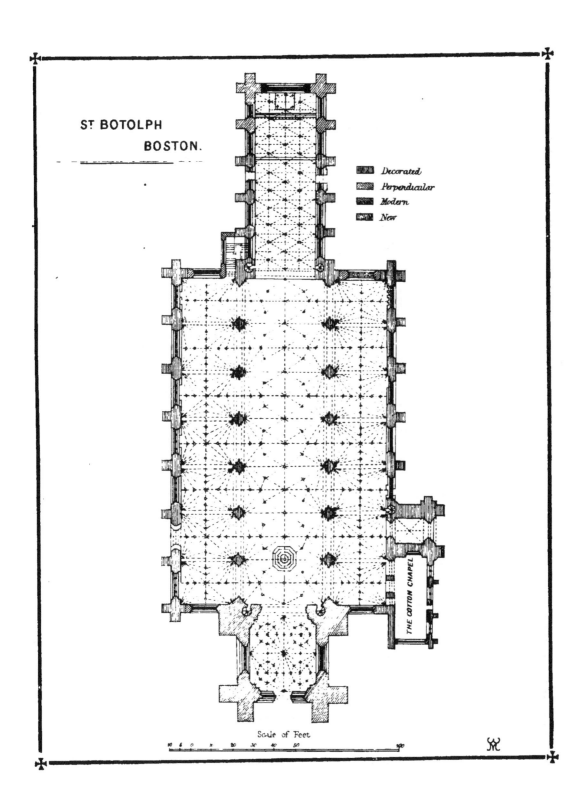

ST BOTOLPH
BOSTON.

Decorated
Perpendicular
Modern
New

THE COTTON CHAPEL

Scale of Feet

10 5 0   10   20   30   40   50   100

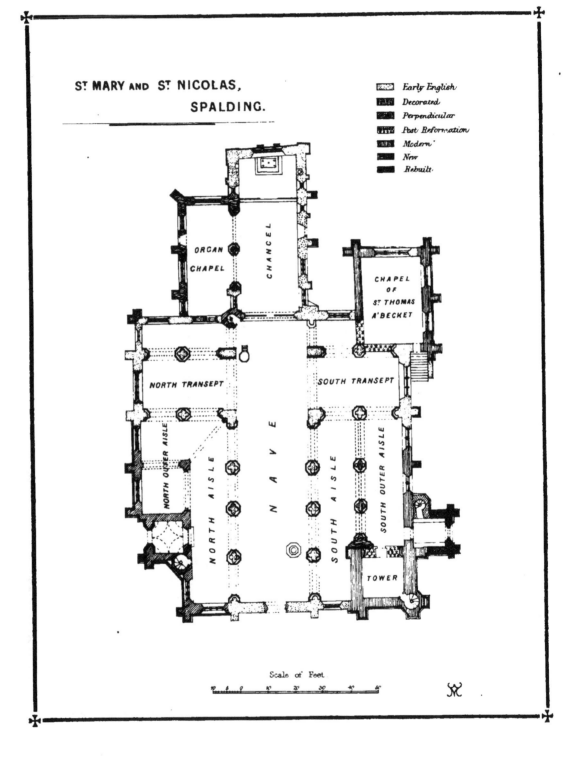

ST MARY AND ST NICOLAS,
SPALDING.

Early English
Decorated
Perpendicular
Post Reformation
Modern
New
Rebuilt

ORGAN CHAPEL

CHANCEL

CHAPEL OF ST THOMAS A'BECKET

NORTH TRANSEPT

SOUTH TRANSEPT

NORTH OUTER AISLE

NORTH AISLE

N A V E

SOUTH AISLE

SOUTH OUTER AISLE

TOWER

Scale of Feet
10 5 0   10   20   30   40   50

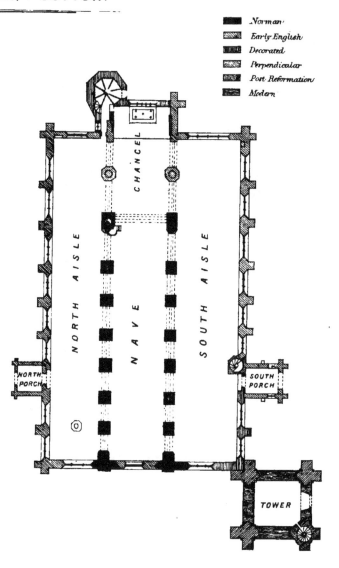

ST MARY, SUTTON.

Norman
Early English
Decorated
Perpendicular
Post Reformation
Modern

CHANCEL

NORTH AISLE

NAVE

SOUTH AISLE

NORTH PORCH

SOUTH PORCH

TOWER

Scale of Feet.

10 5 0   10   20   30   40   50

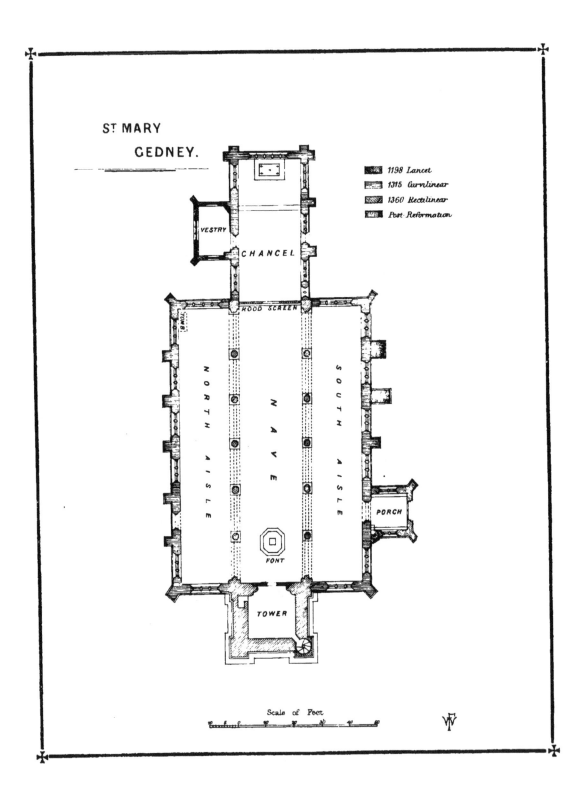

ST MARY

GEDNEY.

1198 Lancet
1315 Curvilinear
1360 Rectilinear
Post-Reformation

VESTRY

CHANCEL

ROOD SCREEN

NORTH AISLE

NAVE

SOUTH AISLE

PORCH

FONT

TOWER

Scale of Feet

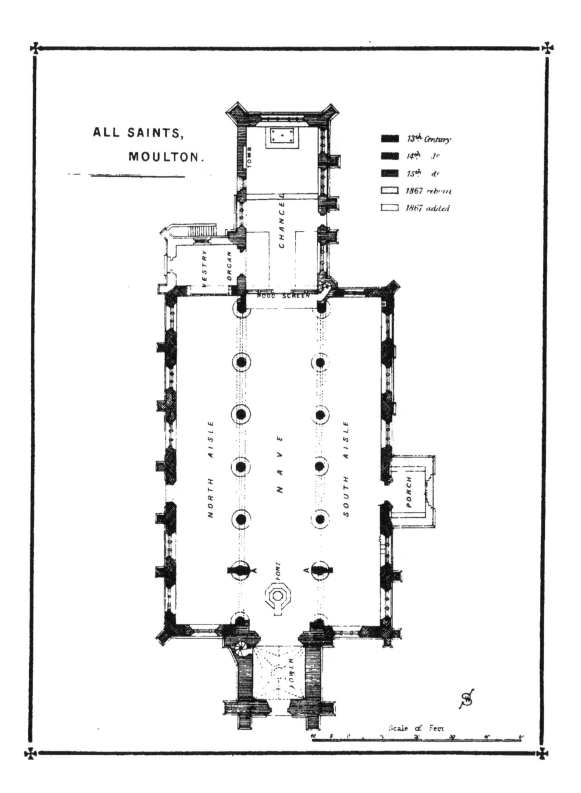

ALL SAINTS,
MOULTON.

13th Century
14th d⁰
15th d⁰
1867 rebuilt
1867 added

TOMB

CHANCEL

VESTRY
ORGAN

WOOD SCREEN

NORTH AISLE

NAVE

SOUTH AISLE

PORCH

FONT

A

TOWER

Scale of Feet
10   5   0   10   20   30   40   50

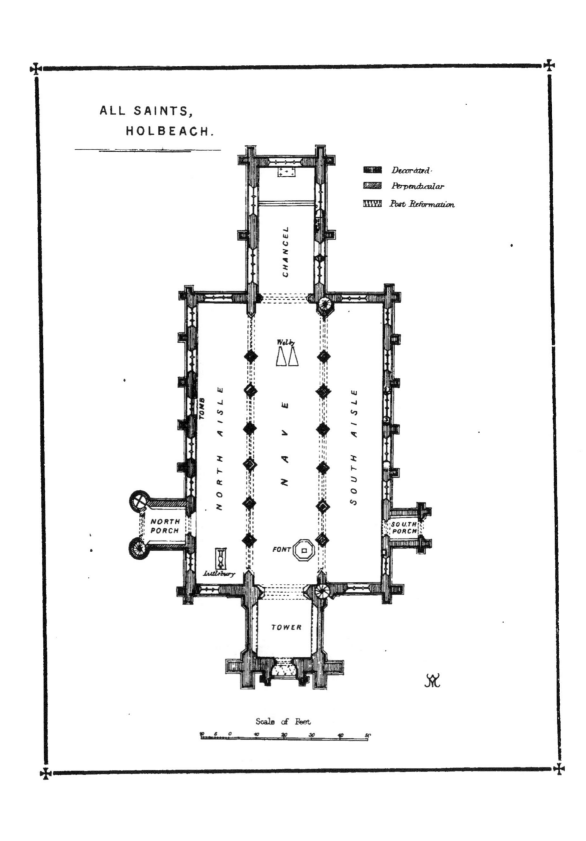

ALL SAINTS,
HOLBEACH.

Decorated
Perpendicular
Post Reformation

CHANCEL

Welby

NORTH AISLE

TOMB

NAVE

SOUTH AISLE

NORTH
PORCH

SOUTH
PORCH

Littlebury

FONT

TOWER

Scale of Feet

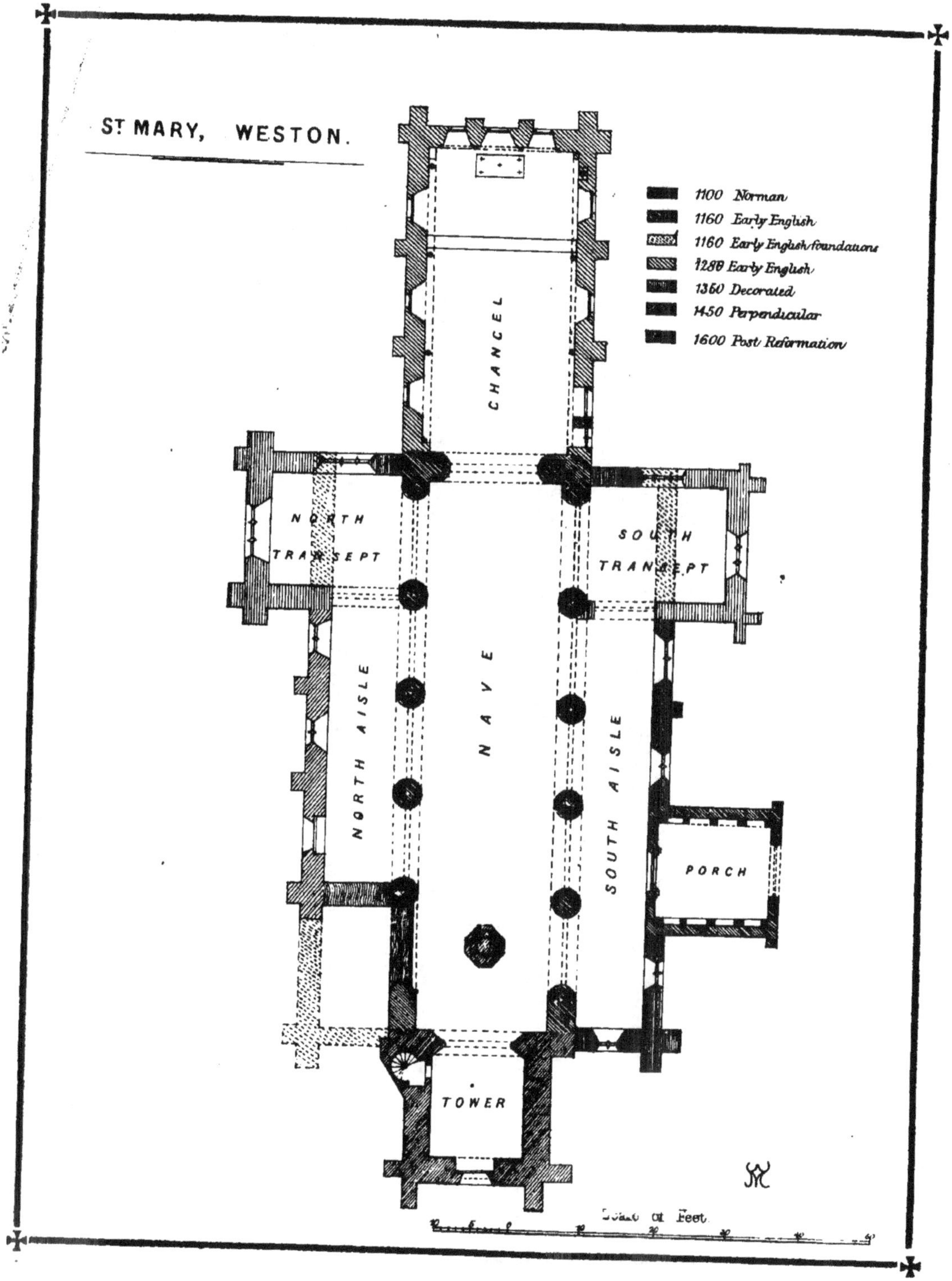
ST MARY, WESTON.
1100 Norman
1160 Early English
1160 Early English foundations
1280 Early English
1360 Decorated
1450 Perpendicular
1600 Post Reformation
CHANCEL
NORTH TRANSEPT
SOUTH TRANSEPT
NORTH AISLE
NAVE
SOUTH AISLE
PORCH
TOWER
Scale of Feet

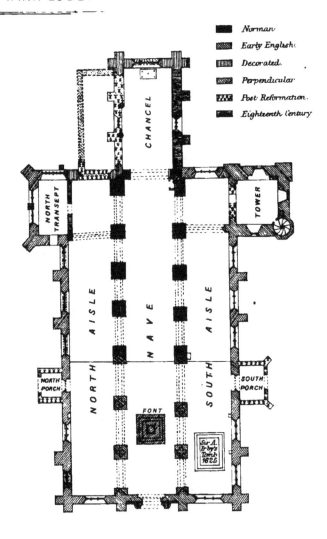

St MARY,
WHAPLODE.

Norman
Early English
Decorated
Perpendicular
Post Reformation
Eighteenth Century

CHANCEL

TOWER

NORTH TRANSEPT

NORTH AISLE

NAVE

SOUTH AISLE

NORTH PORCH

SOUTH PORCH

FONT

Sir A. Irby's Tomb 1625

Scale of Feet

10 5 0   10   20   30   40   50

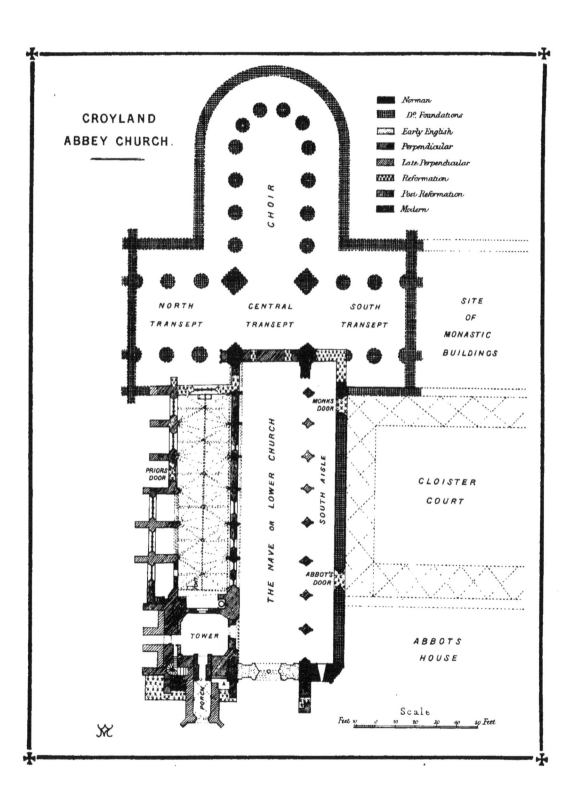

CROYLAND
ABBEY CHURCH.

Norman
Do. Foundations
Early English
Perpendicular
Late Perpendicular
Reformation
Post Reformation
Modern

CHOIR

NORTH
TRANSEPT

CENTRAL
TRANSEPT

SOUTH
TRANSEPT

SITE
OF
MONASTIC
BUILDINGS

MONKS
DOOR

PRIORS
DOOR

THE NAVE OR LOWER CHURCH

SOUTH AISLE

CLOISTER
COURT

ABBOT'S
DOOR

TOWER

ABBOTS
HOUSE

PORCH

Scale
Feet 10   0   10   20   30   40   50 Feet

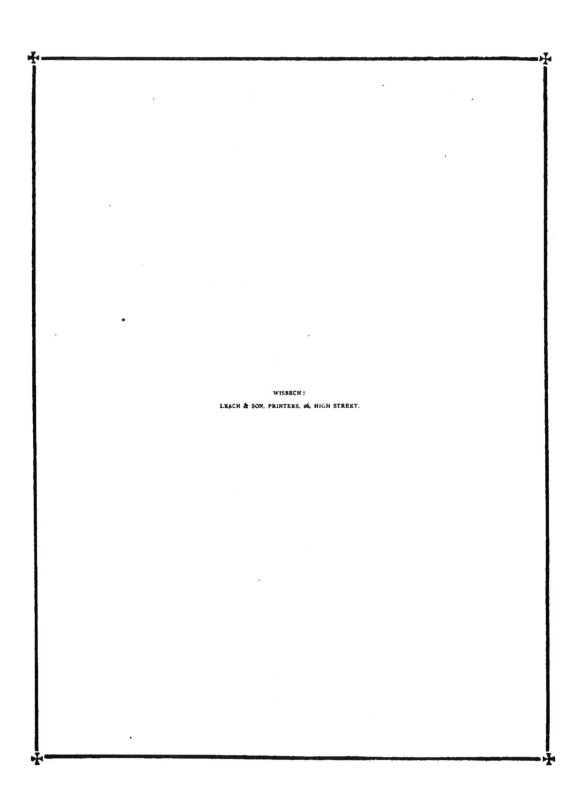

WISBECH:

LEACH & SON, PRINTERS, 26, HIGH STREET.

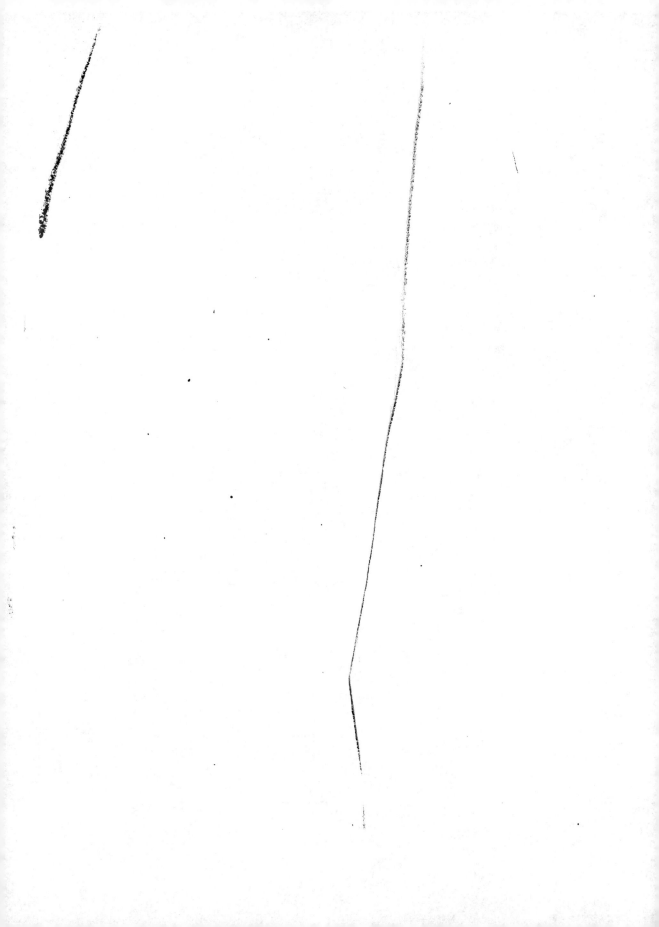

Lightning Source UK Ltd.
Milton Keynes UK
UKHW030629150922
408910UK00006B/567

9 781276 881968